Christmas

Why, Where & When

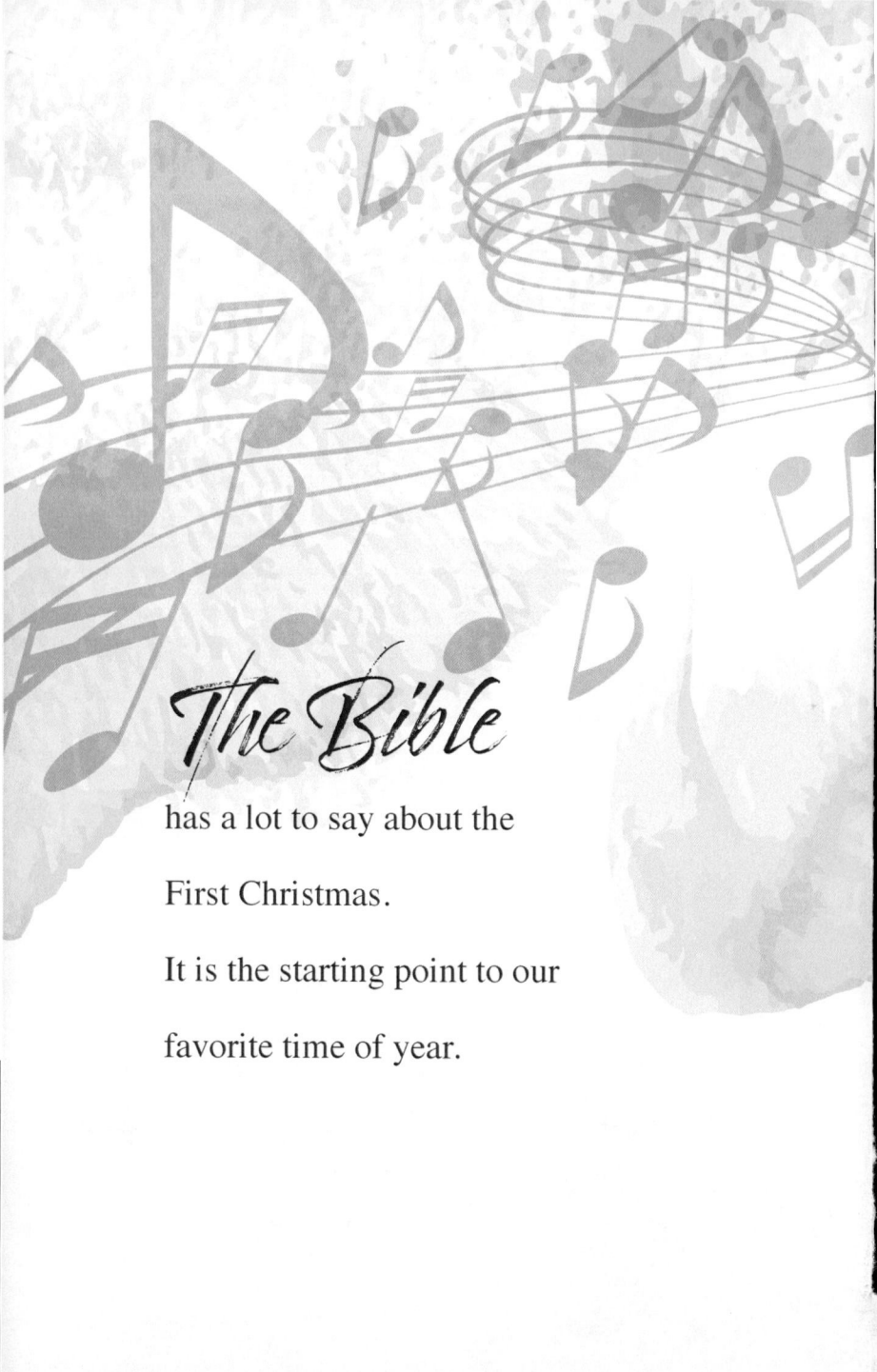

The Bible

has a lot to say about the

First Christmas.

It is the starting point to our

favorite time of year.

The First Noel

means the first Christmas.

The First Noel is also a wonderful song

we sing this time of year about the

baby in a manger.

The baby we know as the Christ Child.

Christ means anointed one

Jesus was born that holy night. He was God's son who became flesh, sent by His Father to save us from our sins and show us a better way.

Sin was brought into this world by Adam and Eve's disobedience toward God in the Garden of Eden. Death also came into the world that dark day. *But God* had a plan.

That First Noel

has been overlooked by many, and yet it is

why Christmas is Christmas today.

In the New Testament of the Bible, the book

of Luke, chapters 1 and 2, tells the story of

the first gift of Christmas: *Jesus.*

Mankind has done its best to turn this *holy season* into a buying and selling fest. Squelching the true meaning.

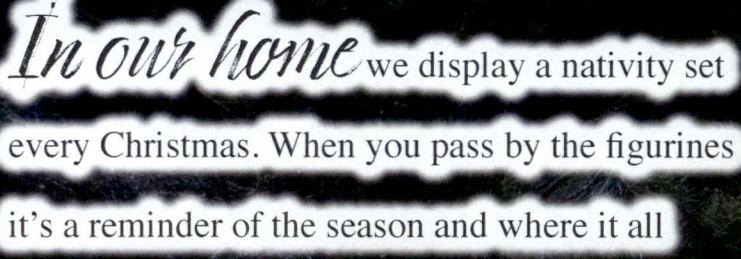*In our home* we display a nativity set every Christmas. When you pass by the figurines it's a reminder of the season and where it all began. Sometimes I stop to ponder Mary and Joseph, and what they were going through. No modern conveniences, the Romans were forcing them to travel to their hometown to be registered. Trying to find a nice place for Mary to give birth, but ending up in a stable for animals. No family or friends to help.

These were ancient people living in an ancient time. But they were still just as real as we are today.

As you go through the busyness of the Christmas season, stop now and then to remember Mary and Joseph and the road they traveled so long ago.

Why would God devise such an elaborate plan? *Because He loved us.*

*Bethlehem.* The name means house of bread. Jesus was proclaimed, later in His ministry, to be the Bread of Life. But for now in our story it is the birthplace of our King, and a humble King at that.

How did Bethlehem become the birthplace?

Rome was under the rule of Caeser Augustus at that time and he declared that everyone must return to the place of their family's origin for the census. The reason for this was taxation, more income for the Roman Empire.

Jesus' birth was around
4-6 BC which was the first
century and the time of King
Herod's reign.
Joseph was of the house and
lineage of King David, which
originates in Bethlehem.
Mary, being betrothed to him,
traveled with Joseph to be
registered for the census.

Biblical scholars say the distance from Nazareth, where Mary and Joseph lived, to Bethlehem, was approximately 90 miles. It would have been a difficult walk of challenging terrain and dangerous due to wild animals and criminals.

According to the scholars, to travel 90 miles would have taken four days of walking eight hours a day. A lot went into that first Christmas.

So, a small town in Judea called Bethlehem became the birthplace of Jesus.

Thirty-three years

later He took our sins

upon Himself, when He died

on a Roman cross.

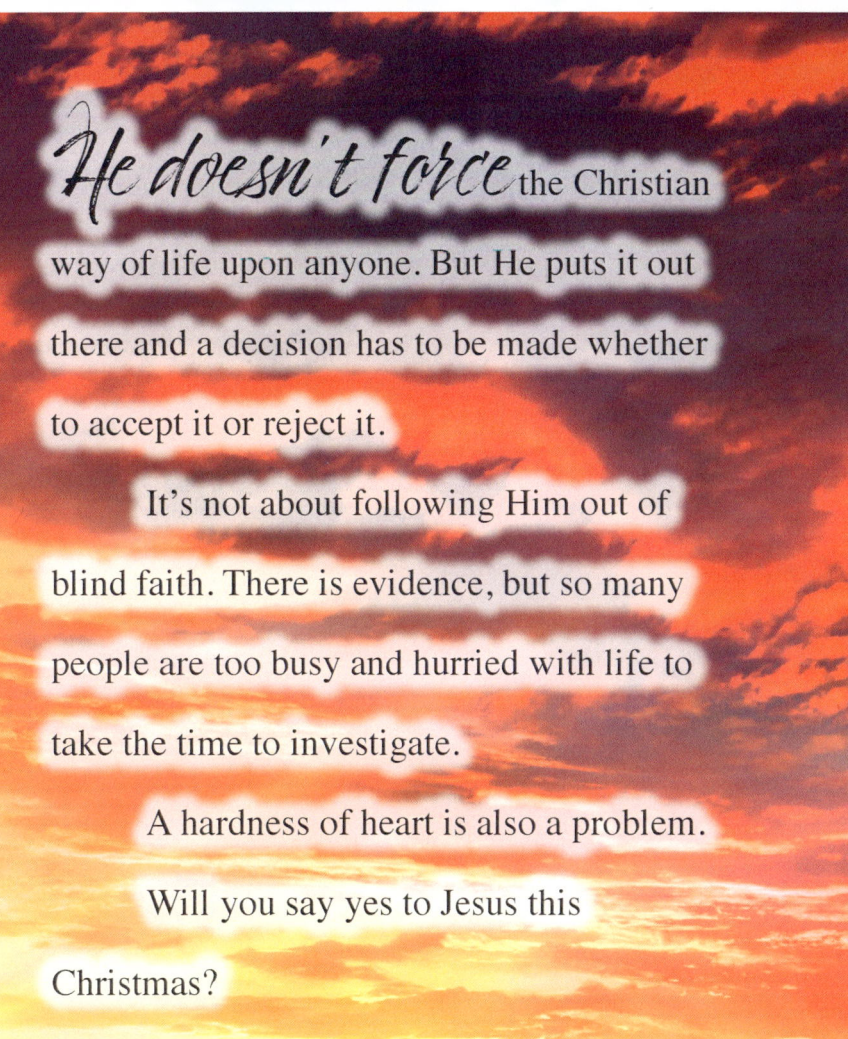

He doesn't force the Christian way of life upon anyone. But He puts it out there and a decision has to be made whether to accept it or reject it.

It's not about following Him out of blind faith. There is evidence, but so many people are too busy and hurried with life to take the time to investigate.

A hardness of heart is also a problem.

Will you say yes to Jesus this Christmas?

Saying Yes to Jesus is as easy as

whispering this little prayer:

Dear God, I know I'm a sinner, and I ask for Your forgiveness. I believe Jesus Christ is Your Son. I believe that He died for my sin and that You raised Him to life. I want to trust Him as my Savior and follow Him as Lord. Guide my life and help me to do your will. Amen

One of the best movies and most realistic we have seen that tells the story of Jesus' birth and the First Christmas is called *The Nativity*. We watch it each year and it makes a great and meaningful addition to Christmas family traditions.

Merry Christmas

CHRISTMAS: WHY, WHERE & WHEN

© 2025 Steve Kukla
Published by S&S Publishing, Inc.
www.sspublishinginc.com

ISBN: 979-8-9931868-0-1

Printed In The United States Of America